SEV NATURAL WONDERS OF THE WORLD

Raymond Coutu

Contents

Rigby

A Harcourt Achieve Imprint

www.Rigby.com

1-800-531-5015

Natural Wonders of the World

The pyramids of Egypt, the Great Wall of China, and the Taj Mahal of India are structures that some experts call "wonders of the world." What makes these structures so amazing is that they were built long ago, when modern-day construction tools and machines were not available. Builders had to rely on their knowledge and strength.

However, there are natural wonders, too— wonders that were formed not by humans, but by the forces of nature, such as blowing wind, shifting glaciers, and flowing lava. These wonders include canyons, waterfalls, reefs, mountains, and even a crater created by a **meteorite** that struck the earth 50,000 years ago.

Paci Ocea

Many people from all around the world visit the Taj Mahal and the pyramids of Egypt each year.

Where in the World Are the Seven Natural Wonders?

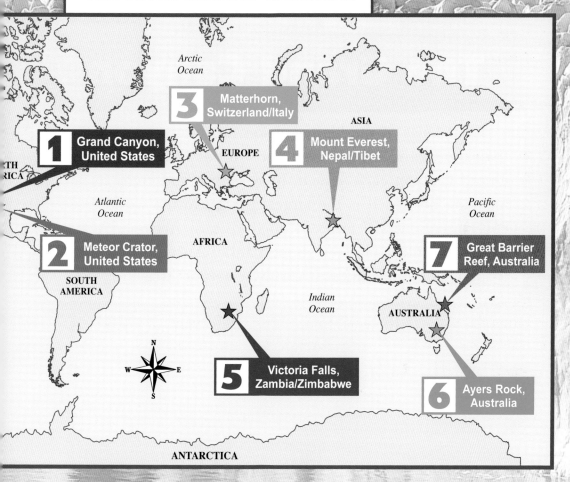

3 Matterhorn, Switzerland/Italy

1 Grand Canyon, United States

4 Mount Everest, Nepal/Tibet

2 Meteor Crator, United States

7 Great Barrier Reef, Australia

5 Victoria Falls, Zambia/Zimbabwe

6 Ayers Rock, Australia

Arctic Ocean

ASIA

EUROPE

Atlantic Ocean

Pacific Ocean

AFRICA

NORTH AMERICA

SOUTH AMERICA

Indian Ocean

AUSTRALIA

ANTARCTICA

N W E S

1

The Grand Canyon

Few places in the United States are more awe-inspiring than the Grand Canyon. Millions of people visit the Grand Canyon each year to hike, camp, and enjoy its amazing beauty. It is the largest **gorge** in the world, covering about 277 miles of northwestern Arizona. At its deepest point, it plunges about 1 mile. At its widest point, it spans about 18 miles. It's truly a natural treasure.

How Was the Grand Canyon Formed?

If you think that rivers are just pleasant places to fish and swim, think again. A single river helped to create the Grand Canyon. For about five million years, since **prehistoric** times, the Colorado River has been flowing through the gorge, chipping away at the earth to reveal multicolored layers of rock and creating massive walls, peaks, and **plateaus**.

One of the Grand Canyon's most beautiful features is the stripes of oranges, reds, grays, and browns found in the canyon walls. As the Colorado River has cut into the land, it has revealed layer upon layer of limestone, sandstone, shale, and other types of rock. These beautiful layers reveal evidence of ancient seas and deserts, **extinct** plants and animals, volcanic eruptions, and earthquakes.

Ancient Art

The Anasazi inhabited the Grand Canyon from about 200 B.C. to 1300 A.D., long before Spanish explorers arrived. Remarkable evidence of the Anasazi civilization remains, including bits of broken pottery, village ruins, and cave drawings like this one.

Exploration of the Grand Canyon began in the sixteenth century, when Spanish explorers arrived in search of gold. The **terrain** proved too dangerous for them, and the expedition was a failure.

In 1869, three centuries later, Major John Wesley Powell, a U.S. officer in the Civil War, led the first expedition to map the canyon. He had a serious handicap: seven years earlier, he had lost his right arm in battle.

Powell started out with nine men and four boats. Within a short time, the rapids, cliffs, and extreme weather took their toll. One boat was lost, and three men quit. But Powell pushed on to become the first person to explore the entire length of the glorious Grand Canyon.

To map the entire length of the Grand Canyon, which is nearly 300 miles, John Wesley Powell (the man in the middle) and his team faced many dangers before successfully completing their expedition.

2 Meteor Crater

You don't have to go to the moon to find craters. In fact, if you live near Winslow, Arizona, you have one right in your backyard. Meteor Crater was formed when a 300,000-ton meteorite slammed into the earth about 50,000 years ago.

How Was Meteor Crater Formed?

The meteorite most likely hit the earth's atmosphere at about 32,000 miles per hour. The impact with the earth was equal to 2½ megatons of TNT exploding and produced winds of more than 600 miles per hour. (By comparison, at landfall, Hurricane Katrina was producing winds of 140 miles per hour.) Any plants and animals within 2 miles of ground zero were probably killed instantly. The 570-foot-deep, 4,180-foot-wide hole is all that is left.

How Meteor Crater was formed was a topic of great scientific debate. Until the early part of the twentieth century, most scientists believed **geologist** Grove Karl Gilbert's theory that it was formed not by a meteorite's impact, but by a massive explosion of steam deep within the earth.

Then Daniel Moreau Barringer stepped forward with his own theory. Using better testing methods, Barringer discovered that the earth inside and around the crater contained iron oxide, which is a common part of meteorites. He also studied the physical shape of the crater and concluded that it was created from a tremendously violent force acting from outside the earth, not inside.

Scientists estimate that the meteorite that created Meteor Crater struck about 50,000 years ago, which might seem like ancient history. However, in comparison, the meteorite that may have caused the dinosaurs to become extinct struck about 65 million years ago.

Could It Happen Again?

According to scientists' best guesses, major meteorite strikes occur about every 1,000 years. The most recent one may have been the Tunguska explosion of 1908, which destroyed a Siberian forest about the size of Rhode Island.

Thousands of trees were uprooted and flattened by the Tunguska explosion of 1908.

But what happened to the meteorite itself? Barringer believed that it had plunged into the earth and was buried beneath the crater. However, astronomer F. R. Moulton determined that the meteorite had, in fact, vaporized on impact, leaving behind the immense crater that so many people have found fascinating.

3

The Matterhorn

At 14,692 feet, the Matterhorn is about half the height of Mount Everest, the world's tallest mountain. But what the Matterhorn lacks in height it makes up for in beauty. It's like an enormous, modern sculpture of an almost perfect pyramid rising up against the sky. Artists and adventurers have been drawn to the villages surrounding it for generations.

How Was the Matterhorn Formed?

The Matterhorn is part of a mountain system called the Alps. The Alps were created by active **glaciers**, which are enormous sheets of ice that scrape rock from the earth as they melt, expand, and change shape over time. The Matterhorn's distinctive shape is the result of glaciers pushing inward from opposite sides of the mountain and wearing away at its surfaces.

Despite the Matterhorn's fame and beauty, it is not the tallest mountain of the Alps. In fact, it is not even in the top 100 tallest mountains of the Alps. Several neighboring mountains, such as Monte Rosa and the Weisshorn, have higher peaks. Though these peaks were all sculpted by glaciers, the Matterhorn stands out as the most remarkable looking. Most scientists believe that after the last ice age ended, the climate changed so quickly that the glaciers were absorbed back into the mountains in less than 300 years.

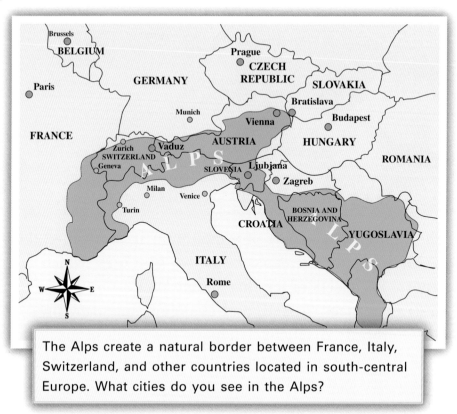

The Alps create a natural border between France, Italy, Switzerland, and other countries located in south-central Europe. What cities do you see in the Alps?

Glaciers can still be found in the Alps, but they have been melting at a rapid rate since 1980 due to global warming. Some scientists fear that the glaciers in the Alps will be almost completely gone in the next fifty years. In response, Austrian researchers are "wrapping the glaciers," or covering the glaciers with a fabric designed to preserve the ice.

No Melting Allowed!

White fleece is used to wrap glaciers in an attempt to slow the melting process of the snow and ice. In the summer of 2005, a glacier at a popular ski resort in Austria was covered with nearly 25 acres of fleece.

The Matterhorn's steep faces and common **avalanches** prevented even the most experienced climbers from attempting to climb to its peak. However, on July 14, 1865, Edward Whymper and a team of six men reached the top. The Matterhorn was the last major mountain of the Alps to be climbed.

It was a tragic victory. On the way down, one man slipped. Because the entire team was roped together, three other men were pulled down with him. All four men began sliding down the mountain's face. The three men who remained standing, including Whymper, attempted a rescue, but the rope snapped, sending the four men to their deaths 4,000 feet below. The broken rope is on display at a small museum in Zermatt, the town at the base of the mountain. Since that tragic day, though, many people have successfully climbed the immense mountain.

Whymper's team followed the Hörnli route, which begins on the Swiss side of the mountain, rather than the more commonly attempted southern route from the Italian side. The climb was easier than expected, and the team made it quickly and smoothly.

Climbing into History

Men weren't the only early mountain climbers. For over 21 years, Lucy Walker climbed many of the tallest mountains in the Alps. Her greatest success came in 1871, when she became the first woman to reach the Matterhorn's peak. Amazingly enough, Walker made all of her climbs wearing a dress because, at that time, it was considered unladylike for a woman to wear anything else!

Even though women in the nineteenth century were expected to always wear a dress, some would wear riding pants while making their dangerous climbs.

4

Mount Everest

Mount Everest is part of the Himalaya Mountain Range, located along the border of Nepal and Tibet. Rising about 29,035 feet above sea level, this mountain is the highest on the earth. Temperatures can dip as low as -76°F on its icy cliffs.

How Was Mount Everest Formed?

The earth's outer shell is made of plates that fit together like enormous jigsaw-puzzle pieces. About 45 million years ago, two plates in Asia began pressing together because of the movement of molten rock deep within the earth. As a result, the plates buckled and forced the earth's crust to rise up, forming the Himalaya Mountain Range, with Mount Everest at its highest point. The two plates are still pressing against each other—each year, the height of the mountains grows about two inches!

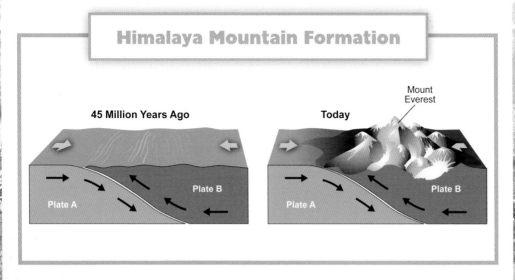

Himalaya Mountain Formation

45 Million Years Ago

Plate B

Plate A

Today

Mount Everest

Plate B

Plate A

Who was the first person to reach the peak of Mount Everest? The answer isn't clear. On June 6, 1924, Englishmen George Leigh Mallory and Andrew Irvine began their climb. On June 8, they vanished in a storm and were never heard from again. Seventy-five years later, in 1999, a group of U.S. climbers found Mallory's body, well preserved in the cold, dry air. Doctors determined that Mallory was killed in a fall. However, did he reach the summit before the tragic fall? No one knows.

Mallory and Irvine's attempt to summit Mount Everest ended in tragedy. Both men perished—and it is uncertain whether they reached the top before they died. This is the last photo taken of them.

Attempts to reach the summit were made after Mallory and Irvine's tragedy, but none was successful until May 29, 1953, when Edmund Hillary, a New Zealand beekeeper, and Tenzing Norgay, a Nepalese mountaineer, stepped onto Mount Everest's peak and made history.

The news of Hillary and Norgay successfully climbing Mount Everest was so exciting, it was the main headline instead of the crowning of the new queen.

Altitude Sickness

The air atop Mount Everest has only about one third the oxygen the air at sea level has. Therefore, as one climber put it, hiking up there is like "running on a treadmill and breathing through a straw." **Altitude** sickness, which can be fatal if untreated, can result. The only cure for altitude sickness is to return to a lower altitude. Signs of altitude sickness include:

- headaches
- dizziness
- nausea
- loss of concentration and balance

- visual hallucinations, or seeing things that aren't there
- auditory hallucinations, or hearing things that aren't there
- fluid in the lungs and/or brain

When climbers reach higher altitudes on Mount Everest, they use oxygen masks to avoid the dangers of altitude sickness.

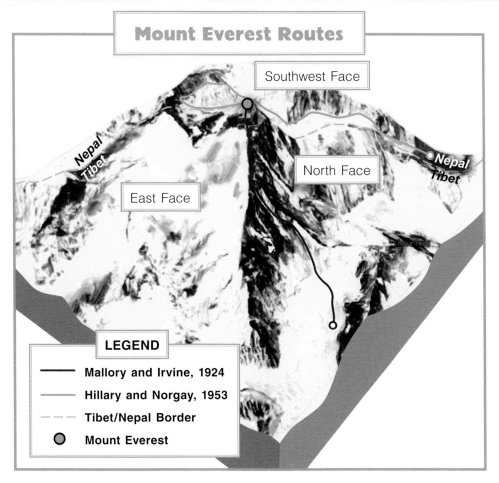

Mount Everest Routes

Southwest Face

North Face

Nepal
Tibet

Nepal
Tibet

East Face

LEGEND

Mallory and Irvine, 1924

Hillary and Norgay, 1953

Tibet/Nepal Border

Mount Everest

Mount Everest has three clearly defined sides: the North Face, the Southwest Face, and the East Face. The edges leading up to the summit are called ridges. Mallory and Irvine began their climb in Tibet and followed the northeast ridge, while Hillary and Norgay began their climb in Nepal and followed the southeast ridge. Both of these routes are still being used by climbers today.

5

Victoria Falls

On southern Africa's Zambezi River between Zimbabwe and Zambia is the stunning Victoria Falls. Above the falls, the Zambezi River runs smoothly and quietly, giving no sign of the awe-inspiring drop to come. At the drop, the water crashes 355 feet into a narrow gorge about 1 mile wide. An average of 130 million gallons of water per minute spills over Victoria Falls—enough to fill about 100 Olympic-size swimming pools!

The falling water generates spray that can rise as high as a mile and a roar that can travel as far as 20 miles. This explains the falls' local name, *Mosi-oa-Tunya*, which translated from Bantu means "smoke that thunders."

How Was Victoria Falls Formed?

The modern-day Zambezi River was actually formed from two prehistoric rivers. Roughly 150 million years ago, the African landscape was covered by molten lava that came from deep within the earth. Over time, cracks formed in the hardened lava and filled with water, creating rivers that led to the ocean. Gradually, parts of the earth's crust rose, changing the course of one of the rivers that would become the modern-day Zambezi River. This river met up with the other river that would form the Zambezi. This combined river fell 820 feet over a cliff, creating the original waterfall. As the centuries passed, the constantly moving water wore away at the soft earth, widening the waterfall and creating the enormous Victoria Falls.

How Does Victoria Falls Compare to Other Famous Waterfalls?

Name	Location	Height	Width
Angel	Venezuela	2,648 feet	350 feet
Niagara	Canada	167 feet	3,948 feet
Victoria	Zambia/Zimbabwe	355 feet	5,700 feet
Yosemite	United States	1,430 feet	93 feet

Human History

In 1855, Scottish missionary David Livingstone traveled the Zambezi River in search of a trade route to the Indian Ocean. He began his journey by walking, but switched to a canoe on the day he encountered the falls. He stopped at an island near

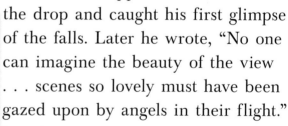

the drop and caught his first glimpse of the falls. Later he wrote, "No one can imagine the beauty of the view . . . scenes so lovely must have been gazed upon by angels in their flight."

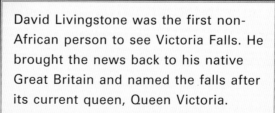

David Livingstone was the first non-African person to see Victoria Falls. He brought the news back to his native Great Britain and named the falls after its current queen, Queen Victoria.

Livingstone spent thirty years exploring Africa. He loved the continent very much. Upon his death in 1873, his body was shipped to England for burial at Westminster Abbey. As he wished, though, one part was left behind for burial in Africa—his heart.

The area around Victoria Falls is now visited frequently by tourists. For the more adventurous traveler, there's a 364-foot bungee jump off of the Victoria Falls railway bridge!

6

Ayers Rock

The grassy desert in central Australia is flat except for a red bump in the earth. It looks like a hill because of its enormous size. But actually it's a rock–Ayers Rock, which rises 1,142 feet high and is 5½ miles around. It's also known as *Uluru*, the name given to it by Aborigines, Australia's native people.

How Was Ayers Rock Formed?

About 550 million years ago, a huge mountain range formed in central Australia. Over the next 50 million years, however, the desert's harsh climate eroded the mountains, leaving behind a plain of **sediment** about 1½-miles thick. Then, about 325 million years ago, the earth's crust shifted, lifting layers of sediment to create the enormous rock.

Ayers Rock is made of arkose, a mixture of sand, quartz, feldspar, and bits of iron oxide. Its red color is the result of a chemical reaction between the iron in the rock and the oxygen in the air.

Ayers Rock appears to change color at different times of the day and year. The minerals in the sandstone of Ayers Rock reflect the red light of the sun during sunrise and sunset, making the rock look as though it's glowing. During rare wet periods, the rock looks silver and gray.

Ayers Rock is a stunning sight, but even more stunning is the fact that it extends $3\frac{1}{2}$ miles below the earth's surface.

Animal Inhabitants

While visiting Ayers Rock, you might see a kangaroo or a dingo, a woma python slithering past, or a thorny devil lizard creeping by in search of shade.

woma python

kangaroo

thorny devil lizard

dingo

English explorer Ernest Giles was the first outsider to lay eyes on what he called "the remarkable pebble." However, William C. Gosse was the first outsider to reach the rock. On July 19, 1873, he climbed to the top of the rock and named it after Sir Henry Ayers, the chief secretary of South Australia at the time.

ERNEST GILES,
The Australian Explorer, Born 1835.

Ernest Giles saw the enormous rock that would come to be called Ayers Rock on an expedition he led across central Australia in 1872.

However, as is the case with many natural wonders, explorers did not "discover" Ayers Rock. Australia's native people did. Originally, Ayers Rock and its surroundings were part of the Petermann Aboriginal Reserve, which the Australian government set aside as a place for Aborigines to live, work, and worship. But in 1958, the government took back the area to create a national park. Aborigines waged an almost 30-year legal battle to regain ownership. In 1985, they won. The Uluru-Kata Tjuta National Park, which includes the amazing Ayers Rock, now belongs to descendants of the people who originally lived there.

Although Ayers Rock is the best known of the park's attractions, visitors are also able to enjoy the beauty of the park's sand dunes, gorges, and rock art.

7 The Great Barrier Reef

The Great Barrier Reef is located a short distance off the coast of northeast Australia. It is not one reef as its name implies, but a 1,240-mile string of more than 3,000 small reefs, or land masses that form just above or below the ocean's surface. **Barrier reefs** are long, narrow, and located close to the mainland's shore, providing protection from the crashing waves of the open ocean.

How Was the Great Barrier Reef Formed?

The Great Barrier Reef is a coral reef, meaning that it is not made up of rock, but of tiny, colorful animals called polyps that look more like plants. Polyps band together to form colonies. As colonies die off, their skeletons form a limestone base upon which new polyps attach themselves. This layering of living and dead colonies is how the coral reef grows.

A wide variety of creatures live in and around the Great Barrier Reef. Some are huge, like the sea turtle whose shell can grow up to four feet long, and some are **microscopic**, like the zooplankton, or tiny creatures, upon which polyps feed. Some are fierce, like the giant moray eel, and some are gentle, like the dugong (or "sea cow" as it's more commonly known). The reef is best known for its brilliant, multicolored fish. More than 1,500 species of fish live there, including parrot fish, angelfish, lionfish, and clownfish.

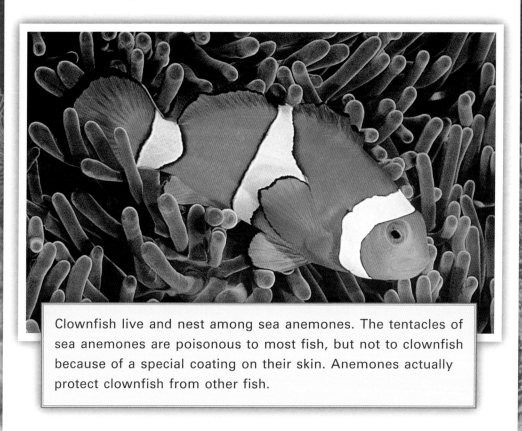

Clownfish live and nest among sea anemones. The tentacles of sea anemones are poisonous to most fish, but not to clownfish because of a special coating on their skin. Anemones actually protect clownfish from other fish.

When the ship *Endeavour* unexpectedly ran into the coast of Australia in 1770, Captain James Cook and his crew had know idea what they had crashed into! The reef was not visible to them, so they had no idea what had happened. They managed to free the ship and get it to the mainland for repairs. They sailed to a nearby island, climbed to the top of a hill, and were shocked by what they saw—miles of coral reef. The crew brought news of the reef back to Great Britain. Not long after that, British settlement of Australia began.

Cook's *Endeavor* Voyage: 1768–1771

The Great Barrier Reef was only one stop along James Cook's three-year journey. He also visited Tahiti, New Guinea, and Batavia, the capital of the Dutch East Indies.

The Great Barrier Reef

Cook's route

AUSTRALIA

PACIFIC OCEAN

June 11, 1770
Grounded by Coral

Coral reefs are so sensitive to their environment that a change in the water temperature range of just a few degrees outside the norm can kill them.

From the late 1800s until very recently, people have been harvesting the Great Barrier Reef's coral for jewelry, its limestone for fertilizer, and its fish for food. In the process, they have been slowly killing the reef. Fortunately, in 1979, the Australian government declared a large part of the reef a national park, protecting it from such threats and allowing future generations to enjoy its amazing beauty.

Is There a Natural Wonder Near You?

These seven natural wonders are, indeed, wondrous, but they are by no means the *only* natural wonders. A natural wonder doesn't have to be a canyon, mountain, or waterfall. It can be a small indoor garden, a neighborhood park, or a favorite tree. Do everything you can to protect these wonders, for they can be destroyed much more quickly than they were created.

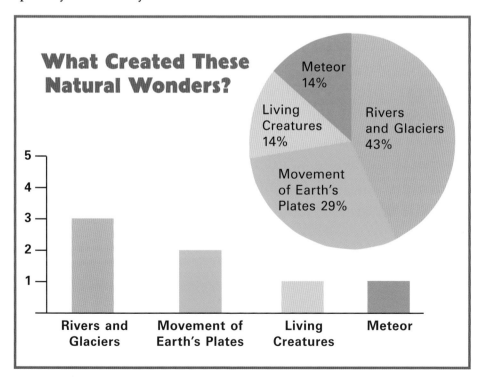

What Created These Natural Wonders?

Meteor 14%

Living Creatures 14%

Rivers and Glaciers 43%

Movement of Earth's Plates 29%

Rivers and Glaciers — 3

Movement of Earth's Plates — 2

Living Creatures — 1

Meteor — 1

Glossary

altitude height above sea level or the earth's surface

avalanche a mass of snow and rocks that quickly slides down a mountain

barrier reef a long, narrow ridge of coral or rock that goes along a coast

extinct no longer existing

geologist a scientist who studies the history and nature of the earth

gorge a deep, narrow pass between steep heights

meteorite a solid body traveling through space that enters the earth's atmosphere and falls to the surface of the planet

microscopic too small to be viewed with the eye

plateau a fairly flat area of land that is higher than the land around it

prehistoric before written history

sediment matter left behind by wind or water

terrain an area of land